The Heidelberg Catechism

ZACHARIUS URSINUS

The Heidelberg Catechism, Z. Ursinus
Jazzybee Verlag Jürgen Beck
86450 Altenmünster, Loschberg 9
Deutschland

ISBN: 9783849678142

Translator: Bishop Henry Parry (1561 -1616)

www.jazzybee-verlag.de
admin@jazzybee-verlag.de

Printed by Createspace, North Charleston, SC, USA

CONTENTS:

OF PRAYER

Note. This Catechism is fully based on the Scriptures. The references to Scripture are indicated in parentheses with a letter. For example, the letter (a) points to the texts (a) placed after the answer.

1. Lord's Day

Question 1.

What is thy only comfort in life and death?

Answer.

That I with body and soul, both in life and death, (a)
am not my own, (b)
but belong unto my faithful Saviour Jesus Christ; (c)
who, with his precious blood, has fully satisfied for all my sins, (d)
and delivered me from all the power of the devil; (e)
and so preserves me (f)
that without the will of my heavenly Father, not a hair can fall from my head; (g)
yea, that all things must be subservient to my salvation, (h)
and therefore, by his Holy Spirit, He also assures me of eternal life, (i)
and makes me sincerely willing and ready, henceforth, to live unto him. (j)

(a) Rom.14:7,8. (b) 1 Cor.6:19. (c) 1 Cor.3:23; Tit.2:14. (d) 1 Pet.1:18,19; 1 John 1:7; 1 John 2:2,12. (e) Heb.2:14; 1 John 3:8; John 8:34-36. (f) John 6:39; John 10:28; 2 Thess.3:3; 1 Pet.1:5. (g) Matt.10:29-31; Luke 21:18. (h) Rom.8:28. (i) 2 Cor.1:20-22; 2 Cor.5:5; Eph.1:13,14; Rom.8:16. (j) Rom.8:14; 1 John 3:3.

Q. 2.

How many things are necessary for thee to know, that thou, enjoying this comfort, mayest live and die happily?

A.

Three; (a)
the first, how great my sins and miseries are; (b)
the second, how I may be delivered from all my sins and miseries; (c)
the third, how I shall express my gratitude to God for such deliverance. (d)

(a) Matt.11:28-30; Luke 24:46-48; 1 Cor.6:11; Tit.3:3-7. (b) John 9:41; John 15:22. (c) John 17:3; Acts 4:12; Acts 10:43. (d) Eph.5:8-11; 1 Pet.2:9,10; Rom.6:1,2,12,13.

THE FIRST PART - OF THE MISERY OF MAN

2. Lord's Day

Q. 3.
Whence knowest thou thy misery?
A.
Out of the law of God. (a)
(a) Rom.3:20.

Q. 4.
What does the law of God require of us?
A.
Christ teaches us that briefly, Matt. 22:37-40, "Thou shalt love the Lord thy God with all thy heart, with all thy soul, and with all thy mind, and with all thy strength. This is the first and the great commandment; and the second is like unto it, Thou shalt love thy neighbour as thyself. On these two commandments hang all the law and the prophets." (a)
(a) Deut.6:5; Lev.19:18; Mark 12:30; Luke 10:27.

Q. 5.
Canst thou keep all these things perfectly?
A.
In no wise; (a)
for I am prone by nature to hate God and my neighbour.(b)
(a) Rom.3:10,20,23; 1 John 1:8,10. (b) Rom.8:7; Eph.2:3; Tit.3:3; Gen.6:5; Gen.8:21; Jer.17:9; Rom.7:23.

3. Lord's Day

Q. 6.
Did God then create man so wicked and perverse?
A.
By no means;
but God created man good, (a)
and after his own image, (b)
in true righteousness and holiness, that he might rightly know God his Creator, heartily love him and live with him in eternal happiness to glorify and praise him. (c)
(a) Gen.1:31. (b) Gen.1:26,27. (c) Col.3:9,10; Eph.4:23,24; 2 Cor.3:18.

Q. 7.

Whence then proceeds this depravity of human nature?

A.

From the fall and disobedience of our first parents,

Adam and Eve, in Paradise; (a)

hence our nature is become so corrupt, that we are all conceived and born in sin. (b)

(a) Gen.3; Rom.5:12,18,19. (b) Ps.51:5; Gen.5:3.

Q. 8.

Are we then so corrupt that we are wholly incapable of doing any good, and inclined to all wickedness?

A.

Indeed we are; (a)

except we are regenerated by the Spirit of God. (b)

(a) Gen.8:21; John 3:6; Gen.6:5; Job 14:4; Job 15:14,16,36; Isa.53:6.

(b) John 3:3,5; 1 Cor.12:3; 2 Cor.3:5.

4. Lord's Day

Q. 9.

Does not God then do injustice to man, by requiring from him in his law, that which he cannot perform?

A.

Not at all; (a)

for God made man capable of performing it;

but man, by the instigation of the devil, (b)

and his own wilful disobedience, (c)

deprived himself and all his posterity of those divine gifts.

(a) Eph.4:24; Eccl.7:29. (b) John 8:44; 2 Cor.11:3; Gen.3:4. (c) Gen.3:6; Rom.5:12; Gen.3:13; 1 Tim.2:13,14.

Q. 10.

Will God suffer such disobedience and rebellion to go unpunished?

A.

By no means;

but is terribly displeased (a)

with our original as well as actual sins; and will punish them in his just judgment temporally and eternally, (b)

as he has declared, "Cursed is every one that continueth not in all things, which are written in the book of the law, to do them." (c)

(a) Gen.2:17; Rom.5:12. (b) Ps.5:5; Ps.50:21; Nah.1:2; Exod.20:5; Exod.34:7; Rom.1:18; Eph.5:6; Heb.9:27. (c) Deut.27:26; Gal.3:10.

Q. 11.

Is not God then also merciful?

A.

God is indeed merciful, (a)

but also just; (b)

therefore his justice requires, that sin which is committed against the most high majesty of God, be also punished with extreme, that is, with everlasting punishment of body and soul.

(a) Exod.34:6,7; Exod.20:6. (b) Ps.7:9; Exod.20:5; Exod.23:7; Exod.34:7; Ps.5:5,6; Nah.1:2,3.

THE SECOND PART - OF MAN'S DELIVERANCE

5. Lord's Day

Q. 12.

Since then, by the righteous judgment of God, we deserve temporal and eternal punishment, is there no way by which we may escape that punishment, and be again received into favour?

A.

God will have his justice satisfied: (a)

and therefore we must make this full satisfaction, either by ourselves, or by another. (b)

(a) Gen.2:17; Exod.20:5; Exod.23:7; Ezek.18:4; Matt.5:26; 2 Thess.1:6; Luke 16:2. (b) Rom.8:3,4.

Q. 13.

Can we ourselves then make this satisfaction?

A.

By no means;

but on the contrary we daily increase our debt. (a)

(a). Job 9:2,3; Job 15:15,16; Job 4:18,19; Ps.130:3; Matt.6:12; Matt.18:25; Matt.16:26.

Q. 14.

Can there be found anywhere, one, who is a mere creature, able to satisfy for us?

A.

None; for, first, God will not punish any other creature for the sin which man has committed; (a)

and further, no mere creature can sustain the burden of God's eternal wrath against sin, so as to deliver others from it. (b)

(a) Ezek.18:4; Gen.3:17; Heb.2:14-17. (b) Nah.1:6; Ps.130:3.

Q. 15.

What sort of a mediator and deliverer then must we seek for?

A.

For one who is very man, and perfectly (a)

righteous; (b)

and yet more powerful than all creatures; that is, one who is also very God. (c)

(a) 1 Cor.15:21; Jer.33:16; Isa.53:9; 2 Cor.5:21. (b) Heb.7:16,26. (c) Isa.7:14; Isa.9:6; Rom.9:5; Jer.23:5,6; Jer.23:6; Luke 11:22.

6. Lord's day

Q. 16.
Why must he be very man, and also perfectly righteous?
A.
Because the justice of God requires that the same human nature which has sinned, should likewise make satisfaction for sin; (a) and one, who is himself a sinner, cannot satisfy for others. (b)
(a) Ezek.18:4,20; Rom.5:12,15,18; 1 Cor.15:21; Heb.2:14-16; 1 Pet.3:18; Isa.53:3-5,10,11. (b) Heb.7:26,27; Ps.49:7,8; 1 Pet.3:18.

Q. 17.
Why must he in one person be also very God?
A.
That he might,
by the power of his Godhead (a)
sustain in his human nature, (b)
the burden of God's wrath; (c)
and might obtain for, and restore to us, righteousness and life. (d)
(a) Isa.9:6; Isa.63:3. (b) Isa.53:4,11. (c) Deut.4:24; Nah.1:6; Ps.130:3. (d) Isa.53:5,11; Acts 2:24; 1 Pet.3:18; John 3:16; Acts 20:28; John 1:4.

Q. 18.
Who then is that Mediator, who is in one person both very God, (a)
and a real (b)
righteous man? (c)
A.
Our Lord Jesus Christ: (d)
"who of God is made unto us wisdom, and righteousness, and sanctification, and redemption." (e)
(a) 1 John 5:20; Rom.9:5; Rom.8:3; Gal.4:4; Isa.9:6; Jer.23:6; Mal.3:1. (b) Luke 1:42; Luke 2:6,7; Rom.1:3; Rom.9:5; Philip.2:7; Heb.2:14,16,17; Heb.4:15. (c) Isa.53:9,11; Jer.23:5; Luke 1:35; John 8:46; Heb.4:15; Heb.7:26; 1 Pet.1:19; 1 Pet.2:22; 1 Pet.3:18. (d) 1 Tim.2:5; Heb.2:9; Matt.1:23; 1 Tim.3:16; Luke 2:11. (e) 1 Cor.1:30.

Q. 19.
Whence knowest thou this?
A.
From the holy gospel, which God himself first revealed in Paradise; (a)
and afterwards published by the patriarchs (b)
and prophets, (c)

and represented by the sacrifices and other ceremonies of the law; (d) and lastly, has fulfilled it by his only begotten Son. (e)

(a) Gen.3:15. (b) Gen.22:18; Gen.12:3; Gen.49:10,11. (c) Isa.53; Isa.42:1-4; Isa.43:25; Isa.49:5,6,22,23; Jer.23:5,6; Jer.31:32,33; Jer.32:39-41; Mic.7:18-20; Acts 10:43; Rom.1:2; Heb.1:1; Acts 3:22-24; Acts 10:43; John 5:46. (d) Heb.10:1,7; Col.2:7; John 5:46. (e) Rom.10:4; Gal.4:4,5; Gal.3:24; Col.2:17.

7. Lord's Day

Q. 20.

Are all men then, as they perished in Adam, saved by Christ?

A.

No; (a)

only those who are ingrafted into him, and, receive all his benefits, by a true faith. (b)

(a) Matt.7:14; Matt.22:14. (b) Mark 16:16; John 1:12; John 3:16,18,36; Isa.53:11; Ps.2:12; Rom.11:17,19,20; Rom.3:22; Heb.4:2,3; Heb.5:9; Heb.10:39; Heb.11:6.

Q. 21.

What is true faith?

A.

True faith is not only a certain knowledge, whereby I hold for truth all that God has revealed to us in his word, (a)

but also an assured confidence, (b)

which the Holy Ghost (c)

works by the gospel in my heart; (d)

that not only to others, but to me also, remission of sin, everlasting righteousness and salvation, (e)

are freely given by God, merely of grace, only for the sake of Christ's merits. (f)

(a) James 2:19. (b) 2 Cor.4:13; Eph.2:7-9; Eph.3:12; Gal.2:16; Heb.11:1,7-10; Heb.4:16; James 1:6; Matt.16:17; Philip.1:19; Rom.4:16-21; Rom.5:1; Rom.1:16; Rom.10:10,17; Rom.3:24.25. (c) Gal.5:22; Matt.16:17; 2 Cor.4:13; John 6:29; Eph.2:8; Philip.1:19; Acts 16:14. (d) Rom.1:16; Rom.10:17; 1 Cor.1:21; Acts 10:44; Acts 16:14. (e) Rom.1:17; Gal.3:11; Heb.10:10,38; Gal.2:16. (f) Eph.2:8; Rom.3:24; Rom.5:19; Luke 1:77,78.

Q. 22.

What is then necessary for a christian to believe?

A.
All things promised us in the gospel, (a)
which the articles of our catholic undoubted christian faith briefly teach us.
(a) John 20:31; Matt.28:19; Mark 1:15.

Q. 23.
What are these articles?
A.
1. I believe in God the Father, Almighty, Maker of heaven and earth:
2. And in Jesus Christ, his only begotten Son, our Lord:
3. Who was conceived by the Holy Ghost, born of the Virgin Mary:
4. Suffered under Pontius Pilate; was crucified, dead, and buried: He descended into hell:
5. The third day he rose again from the dead:
6. He ascended into heaven, and sitteth at the right hand of God the Father Almighty:
7. From thence he shall come to judge the quick and the dead:
8. I believe in the Holy Ghost:
9. I believe a holy catholic church: the communion of saints:
10. The forgiveness of sins:
11. The resurrection of the body:
12. And the life everlasting.

8. Lord's Day

Q. 24.
How are these articles divided?
A.
Into three parts;
the first is of God the Father, and our creation;
the second of God the Son, and our redemption;
the third of God the Holy Ghost, and our sanctification.

Q. 25.
Since there is but one only divine essence, (a)
why speakest thou of Father, Son, and Holy Ghost?
A.
Because God has so revealed himself in his word, (b)
that these three distinct persons are the one only true and eternal God.
(a) Deut.6:4; Eph.4:6; Isa.44:6; Isa.45:5; 1 Cor.8:4,6. (b) Isa.61.1, Luke 4:18; Gen.1:2,3; Ps.33:6; Isa.48:16; Ps.110:1; Matt.3:16,17; Matt.28:19; 1 John 5:7; Isa.6:1,3; John 14:26; John 15:26; 2 Cor.13:13; Gal.4:6; Eph.2:18; Tit.3:5,6.

9. Lord's Day

Q. 26.

What believest thou when thou sayest, "I believe in God the Father, Almighty, Maker of heaven and earth"?

A.

That the eternal Father of our Lord Jesus Christ (who of nothing made heaven and earth, with all that is in them; (a)

who likewise upholds and governs the same by his eternal counsel and providence) (b)

is for the sake of Christ his Son, my God and my Father; (c)

on whom I rely so entirely, that I have no doubt, but he will provide me with all things necessary for soul and body (d)

and further, that he will make whatever evils he sends upon me, in this valley of tears turn out to my advantage; (e)

for he is able to do it, being Almighty God, (f)

and willing, being a faithful Father. (g)

(a) Gen.1,2; Job 33:4; Job 38,39; Ps.33:6; Acts 4:24; Acts 14:15; Isa.45:7. (b) Matt.10:29; Heb.1:3; Ps.104:27-30; Ps.115:3; Matt.10:29; Eph.1:11. (c) John 1:12; Rom.8:15; Gal.4:5-7; Eph.1:5. (d) Ps.55:23; Matt.6:25,26; Luke 12:22. (e) Rom.8:28. (f) Rom.10:12; Luke 12:22; Rom.8:23; Isa.46:4; Rom.10:12. (g) Matt.6:25-34; Matt.7:9-11.

10. Lord's Day

Q. 27.

What dost thou mean by the providence of God?

A.

The almighty and everywhere present power of God; (a)

whereby, as it were by his hand, he upholds and governs (b)

heaven, earth, and all creatures; so that herbs and grass, rain and drought, (c)

fruitful and barren years, meat and drink, health and sickness, (d)

riches and poverty, (e)

yea, and all things come, not by chance, but be his fatherly hand. (f)

(a) Acts 17:25-28; Jer.23:23,24; Isa.29:15,16; Ezek.8:12. (b) Heb.1:3. (c) Jer.5:24; Acts 14:17. (d) John 9:3. (e) Prov.22:2. (f) Matt.10:20; Prov.16:33.

Q. 28.

What advantage is it to us to know that God has created, and by his providence does still uphold all things?

A.

That we may be patient in adversity; (a)

thankful in prosperity; (b)

and that in all things, which may hereafter befall us, we place our firm trust in our faithful God and Father, (c)

that nothing shall separate us from his love; (d)

since all creatures are so in his hand, that without his will they cannot so much as move. (e)

(a) Rom.5:3; James 1:3; Ps.39:9; Job 1:21,22. (b) Deut.8:10;
1 Thess.5:18. (c) Ps.55:22; Rom.5:4. (d) Rom.8:38,39. (e) Job 1:12;
Job 2:6; Acts 17:25,28; Prov.21:1.

OF GOD THE SON

11. Lord's Day

Q. 29.

Why is the Son of God called "Jesus", that is a Saviour?

A.

Because he saveth us,

and delivereth us from our sins; (a)

and likewise, because we ought not to seek, neither can find salvation in any other. (b)

(a) Matt.1:21; Heb.7:24,25. (b) Acts 4:12; John 15:4,5; 1 Tim.2:5; Isa.43:11; 1 John 5:11.

Q. 30.

Do such then believe in Jesus the only Saviour, who seek their salvation and welfare of saints, of themselves, or anywhere else?

A.

They do not;

for though they boast of him in words, yet in deeds they deny Jesus the only deliverer and Saviour; (a)

for one of these two things must be true, that either Jesus is not a complete Saviour; or that they, who by a true faith receive this Saviour, must find all things in him necessary to their salvation. (b)

(a) 1 Cor.1:13,30,31; Gal.5:4. (b) Heb.12:2; Isa.9:6; Col.1:19,20; Col.2:10; 1 John 1:7,16.

12. Lord's Day

Q. 31.

Why is he called "Christ", that is anointed?

A.

Because he is ordained of God the Father, and anointed with the Holy Ghost, (a)

to be our chief Prophet and Teacher, (b)

who has fully revealed to us the secret counsel and will of God concerning our redemption; (c)

and to be our only High Priest, (d)

who by the one sacrifice of his body, has redeemed us, (e)

and makes continual intercession with the Father for us; (f)

and also to be our eternal King, who governs us by his word and Spirit, and who defends and preserves us in that salvation, he has purchased for us. (g)

(a) Heb.1:9; Ps.45:8; Isa.61:1; Luke 4:18. (b) Deut.18:15; Acts 3:22; Acts 7:37; Isa.55:4. (c) John 1:18; John 15:15. (d) Ps.110:4. (e) Heb.10:12,14; Heb.9:12,14,28. (f) Rom.8:34; Heb.9:24; 1 John 2:1; Rom.5:9,10. (g) Ps.2:6; Zech.9:9; Matt.21:5; Luke 1:33; Matt.28:18; John 10:28; Rev.12:10,11.

Q. 32.

But why art thou called a Christian? (a)

A.

Because I am a member of Christ by faith, (b)
and thus am partaker of his anointing; (c)
that so I may confess his name, (d)
and present myself a living sacrifice of thankfulness to him: (e)
and also that with a free and good conscience I may fight against sin and Satan in this life (f)
and afterwards I reign with him eternally, over all creatures. (g)

(a) Acts 11:26. (b) 1 Cor.6:15. (c) 1 John 2:27; Acts 2:17. (d) Matt.10:32; Rom.10:10; Mark 8:38. (e) Rom.12:1; 1 Pet.2:5,9; Rev.5:8,10; Rev.1:6. (f) 1 Pet.2:11; Rom.6:12,13; Gal.5:16,17; Eph.6:11; 1 Tim.1:18,19. (g) 2 Tim.2:12; Matt.24:34.

13. Lord's Day

Q. 33.

Why is Christ called the "only begotten Son" of God, since we are also the children of God?

A.

Because Christ alone is the eternal and natural Son of God; (a)
but we are children adopted of God, by grace, for his sake. (b)

(a) John 1:1-3,14,18; Heb.1:1,2; John 3:16; 1 John 4:9; Rom.8:32. (b) Rom.8:15-17; John 1:12; Gal.4:6; Eph.1:5,6.

Q. 34.

Wherefore callest thou him "our Lord"?

A.

Because he hath redeemed us, both soul and body, from all our sins,
not with silver or gold, but with his precious blood, and has delivered us from all the power of the devil; and thus has made us his own property. (a)

(a) 1 Pet.1:18,19; 1 Pet.2:9; 1 Cor.6:20; 1 Cor.7:23; 1 Tim.2:6; John 20:28.

14. Lord's Day

Q. 35.

What is the meaning of these words "He was conceived by the Holy Ghost, born of the virgin Mary"?

A.

That God's eternal Son, who is, and continues (a)

true and eternal God, (b)

took upon him the very nature of man, of the flesh and blood of the virgin Mary, (c)

by the operation of the Holy Ghost; (d)

that he might also be the true seed of David, (e)

like unto his brethren in all things, (f)

sin excepted. (g)

(a) Rom.1:4; Rom.9:5. (b) 1 John 5:20; John 1:1; John 17:3; Rom.1:3; Col.1:15. (c) Gal.4:4; Luke 1:31,42,43. (d) John 1:14; Matt.1:18,20; Luke 1:32,35. (e) Ps.132:11; Rom.1:3; 2 Sam.7:12; Acts 2:30. (f) Philip.2:7; Heb.2:14,17. (g) Heb.4:15.

Q. 36.

What profit dost thou receive by Christ's holy conception and nativity?

A.

That he is our Mediator; (a)

and with His innocence and perfect holiness, covers in the sight of God, my sins, wherein I was conceived and brought forth. (b)

(a) Heb.7:26,27; Heb.2:17. (b) 1 Pet.1:18,19; 1 Pet.3:18; 1 Cor.1:30,31; Rom.8:3,4; Isa.53:11; Ps.32:1.

15. Lord's Day

Q. 37.

What dost thou understand by the words, "He suffered"?

A.

That he, all the time that he lived on earth, but especially at the end of his life, sustained in body and soul, the wrath of God against the sins of all mankind: (a)

that so by his passion, as the only propitiatory sacrifice, (b)

he might redeem our body and soul from everlasting damnation, (c)

and obtain for us the favour of God, righteousness and eternal life. (d)

(a) Isa.53:4; 1 Pet.2:24; 1 Pet.3:18; 1 Tim.2:6. (b) Isa.53:10,12; Eph.5:2; 1 Cor.5:7; 1 John 2:2; 1 John 4:10; Rom.3:25; Heb.9:28; Heb.10:14. (c) Gal.3:13; Col.1:13; Heb.9:12; 1 Pet.1:18,19. (d) Rom.3:25; 2 Cor.5:21; John 3:16; John 6:51; Heb.9:15; Heb.10:19.

Q. 38.

Why did he suffer "under Pontius Pilate, as judge"?

A.

That he, being innocent, and yet condemned by a temporal judge, (a)

might thereby free us from the severe judgement of God to which we were exposed. (b)

(a) John 18:38; Matt.27:24; Acts 4:27,28; Luke 23:14,15; John 19:4.

(b) Ps.69:4; Isa.53:4,5; 2 Cor.5:21; Gal.3:13.

Q. 39.

Is there anything more in his being "crucified", than if he had died some other death?

A.

Yes there is; for thereby I am assured, that he took on him the curse which lay upon me; (a)

for the death of the cross was accursed of God. (b)

(a) Gal.3:13. (b) Deut.21:23.

16. Lord's Day

Q. 40.

Why was it necessary for Christ to humble himself even "unto death"?

A.

Because with respect to the justice and truth of God, (a)

satisfaction for our sins could be made no otherwise, than by the death of the Son of God. (b)

(a) Gen.2:17. (b) Rom.8:3,4; Heb.2:9,14,15.

Q. 41.

Why was he also "buried"?

A.

Thereby to prove that he was really dead. (a)

(a) Matt.27:59,60; Luke 23:52,53; John 19:38-42; Acts 13:29.

Q. 42.

Since then Christ died for us, why must we also die?

A.

Our death is not a satisfaction for our sins, (a)

but only an abolishing of sin, and a passage into eternal life. (b)

(a) Mark 8:37; Ps.49:7. (b) John 5:24; Philip.1:23; Rom.7:24.

Q. 43.

What further benefit do we receive from the sacrifice and death of Christ on the cross?

A.

That by virtue thereof, our old man is crucified, dead and buried with him; (a)

that so the corrupt inclinations of the flesh may no more reign in us; (b)

but that we may offer ourselves unto him a sacrifice of thanksgiving. (c)

(a) Rom.6:6. (b) Rom.6:6-8,11,12; Col.2:12. (c) Rom.12:1.

Q. 44.

Why is there added, "he descended into hell"?

A.

That in my greatest temptations, I may be assured, and wholly comfort myself in this, that my Lord Jesus Christ, by his inexpressible anguish, pains, terrors, and hellish agonies, in which he was plunged during all his sufferings, (a)

but especially on the cross, has delivered me from the anguish and torments of hell. (b)

(a) Ps.18:5,6; Ps.116:3; Matt.26:38; Heb.5:7; Isa.53:10; Matt.27:46.
(b) Isa.53:5.

17. Lord's Day

Q. 45.

What does the "resurrection" of Christ profit us?

A.

First, by his resurrection he has overcome death, that he might make us partakers of that righteousness which he had purchased for us by his death; (a)

secondly, we are also by his power raised up to a new life; (b)

and lastly, the resurrection of Christ is a sure pledge of our blessed resurrection. (c)

(a) 1 Cor.15:16; Rom.4:25; 1 Pet.1:3. (b) Rom.6:4; Col.3:1,3; Eph.2:5,6. (c) 1 Cor.15:12,20,21; Rom.8:11.

18. Lord's Day

Q. 46.

How dost thou understand these words, "he ascended into heaven"?

A.

That Christ, in sight of his disciples, was taken up from earth into heaven; (a)

and that he continues there for our interest, (b)
until he comes again to judge the quick and the dead. (c)
(a) Acts 1:9; Matt.26:64; Mark 16:19; Luke 24:51. (b) Heb.7:25; Heb.4:14; Heb.9:24; Rom.8:34; Eph.4:10; Col.3:1. (c) Acts 1:11; Matt.24:30.

Q. 47.
Is not Christ then with us even to the end of the world, as he has promised? (a)
A.
Christ is very man and very God; with respect to his human nature, he is no more on earth; (b)
but with respect to his Godhead, majesty, grace and spirit, he is at no time absent from us. (c)
(a) Matt.28:20. (b) Heb.8:4; Matt.26:11; John 16:28; John 17:11; Acts 3:21. (c) John 14:17-19; John 16:13; Matt.28:20; Eph.4:8,12.

Q. 48.
But if his human nature is not present, wherever his Godhead is, are not then these two natures in Christ separated from one another?
A.
Not as all, for since the Godhead is illimitable and omnipresent, (a)
it must necessarily follow that the same is beyond the limits of the human nature he assumed, (b)
and yet is nevertheless in this human nature, and remains personally united to it.
(a) Acts 7:49; Jer.23:24. (b) Col.2:9; John 3:13; John 11:15; Matt.28:6.

Q. 49.
Of what advantage to us is Christ's ascension into heaven?
A.
First, that he is our advocate in the presence of his Father in heaven; (a)
secondly, that we have our flesh in heaven as a sure pledge that he, as the head, will also take up to himself, us, his members; (b)
thirdly, that he sends us his Spirit as an earnest, (c)
by whose power we "seek the things which are above, where Christ sitteth on the right hand of God, and not things on earth." (d)
(a) 1 John 2:1; Rom.8:34. (b) John 14:2; John 17:24; John 20:17; Eph.2:6. (c) John 14:16,7; Acts 2:1-4,33; 2 Cor.1:22; 2 Cor.5:5. (d) Col.3:1; Philip.3:14.

19. Lord's Day

Q. 50.

Why is it added,

"and sitteth at the right hand of God"?

A.

Because Christ is ascended into heaven for this end, that he might appear as head of his church, (a)

by whom the Father governs all things. (b)

(a) Eph.1:20,21,23; Col.1:18. (b) Matt.28:18; John 5:22.

Q. 51.

What profit is this glory of Christ, our head, unto us?

A.

First, that by his Holy Spirit he pours out heavenly graces upon us his members; (a)

and then that by his power he defends and preserves us against all enemies. (b)

(a) Acts 2:33; Eph.4:8. (b) Ps.2:9; Ps.110:1,2; John 10:28; Eph.4:8.

Q. 62.

What comfort is it to thee that "Christ shall come again to judge the quick and the dead"?

A.

That in all my sorrows and persecutions, with uplifted head I look for the very same person, who before offered himself for my sake, to the tribunal of God, and has removed all curse from me, to come as judge from heaven: (a)

who shall cast all his and my enemies into everlasting condemnation, (b)

but shall translate me with all his chosen ones to himself, into heavenly joys and glory. (c)

(a) Luke 21:28; Rom.8:23; Philip.3:20; Tit.2:13; 1 Thess.4:16. (b) 2 Thess.1:6,8-10; Matt.25:41-43. (c) Matt.25:34; 2 Thess.1:7.

20. Lord's Day
Q. 53.
What dost thou believe concerning the Holy Ghost?
A.
First, that he is true and coeternal God with the Father and the Son; (a)
secondly, that he is also given me, (b)
to make me by a true faith, partaker of Christ and all his benefits, (c)
that he may comfort me (d)
and abide with me for ever. (e)
(a) 1 John 5:7; Gen.1:2; Isa.48:16; 1 Cor.3:16; 1 Cor.6:19; Acts 5:3,4. (b) Gal.4:6; Matt.28:19,20; 2 Cor.1:21,22; Eph.1:13. (c) Gal.3:14; 1 Pet.1:2; 1 Cor.6:17. (d) Acts 9:31; John 15:26. (e) John 14:16; 1 Pet.4:14.

21. Lord's Day

Q. 54.
What believest thou concerning the "holy catholic church" of Christ?
A.
That the Son of God (a)
from the beginning to the end of the world, (b)
gathers, defends, and preserves (c)
to himself by his Spirit and word, (d)
out of the whole human race, (e)
a church chosen to everlasting life, (f)
agreeing in true faith; (g)
and that I am and forever shall remain, (h)
a living member thereof. (i)
(a) Eph.5:26; John 10:11; Acts 20:28; Eph.4:11-13. (b) Ps.71:17,18; Isa.59:21; 1 Cor.11:26. (c) Matt.16:18; John 10:28-30; Ps.129:1-5. (d) Isa.59:21; Rom.1:16; Rom.10:14-17; Eph.5:26. (e) Gen.26:4; Rev.5:9. (f) Rom.8:29,30; Eph.1:10-13. (g) Acts 2:46; Eph.4:3-6. (h) Ps.23:6; 1 Cor.1:8,9; John 10:28; 1 John 2:19; 1 Pet.1:5. (i) 1 John 3:14,19-21; 2 Cor.13:5; Rom.8:10.

Q. 55.
What do you understand by "the communion of saints"?
A.
First, that all and every one, who believes, being members of Christ, are in common, partakers of him, and of all his riches and gifts; (a)

secondly, that every one must know it to be his duty, readily and cheerfully to employ his gifts, for the advantage and salvation of other members. (b)

(a) 1 John 1:3; 1 Cor.1:9; Rom.8:32; 1 Cor.12:12,13; 1 Cor.6:17. (b) 1Cor.12:21; 1 Cor.13:1,5; Philip.2:4-8.

Q. 56.

What believest thou concerning "the forgiveness of sins"?

A.

That God, for the sake of Christ's satisfaction, will no more remember my sins, neither my corrupt nature, against which I have to struggle all my life long; (a)

but will graciously impute to me the righteousness of Christ, (b)

that I may never be condemned before the tribunal of God. (c)

(a) 1 John 2:2; 1 John 1:7; 2 Cor.5:19,21. (b) Jer.31:34; Ps.103:3,4; Ps.103:10,12; Mic.7:19,23-25. (c) Rom.8:1-4; John 3:18; John 5:24.

22. Lord's Day

Q. 57.

What comfort does the "resurrection of the body" afford thee?

A.

That not only my soul after this life shall be immediately taken up to Christ its head; (a)

but also, that this my body, being raised by the power of Christ, shall be reunited with my soul, and made like unto the glorious body of Christ. (b)

(a) Luke 16:22; Luke 23:43; Philip.1:21,23. (b) 1 Cor.15:53,54; Job 19:25,26; 1 John 3:2; Philip.3:21.

Q. 58.

What comfort takest thou from the article of "life everlasting"?

A.

That

since I now feel in my heart the beginning of eternal joy, (a)

after this life, I shall inherit perfect salvation, which "eye has not seen, nor ear heard, neither has it entered into the heart of man" to conceive, and that to praise God therein for ever. (b)

(a) 2 Cor.5:2,3. (b) 1 Cor.2:9; John 17:3.

23. Lord's Day

Q. 59.

But what does it profit thee now that thou believest all this?

A.

That I am righteous in Christ, before God, and an heir of eternal life. (a)

(a) Hab.2:4; Rom.1:17; John 3:36.

Q. 60.

How are thou righteous before God?

A.

Only by a true faith in Jesus Christ; (a)

so that, though my conscience accuse me, that I have grossly transgressed all the commandments of God, and kept none of them, (b)

and am still inclined to all evil; (c)

notwithstanding, God, without any merit of mine, (d)

but only of mere grace, (e)

grants and imputes to me, (f)

the perfect satisfaction, (g)

righteousness and holiness of Christ; (h)

even so, as if I never had had, nor committed any sin: yea, as if I had fully accomplished all that obedience which Christ has accomplished for me; (i)

inasmuch as I embrace such benefit with a believing heart. (j)

(a) Rom.3:21-25,28; Rom.5:1,2; Gal.2:16; Eph.2:8,9; Philip.3:9. (b) Rom.3:9. (c) Rom.7:23. (d) Tit.3:5; Deut.9:6; Ezek.36:22. (e) Rom.3:24; Eph.2:8. (f) Rom.4:4,5; 2 Cor.5:19. (g) 1 John 2:2. (h) 1 John 2:1. (i) 2 Cor.5:21. (j) Rom.3:22; John 3:18.

Q. 61.

Why sayest thou, that thou art righteous by faith only?

A.

Not that I am acceptable to God, on account of the worthiness of my faith; but because only the satisfaction, righteousness, and holiness of Christ, is my righteousness before God; (a)

and that I cannot receive and apply the same to myself any other way than by faith only. (b)

(a) 1 Cor.1:30; 1 Cor.2:2. (b) 1 John 5:10.

24. Lord's Day

Q. 62.

But why cannot our good works be the whole, or part of our righteousness before God?

A.

Because, that the righteousness, which can be approved of before the tribunal of God, must be absolutely perfect, (a) and in all respects conformable to the divine law; and also, that our best works in this life are all imperfect and defiled with sin. (b)

(a) Gal.3:10; Deut.27:26. (b) Isa.64:6.

Q. 63.

What! do not our good works merit, which yet God will reward in this and in a future life?

A.

This reward is not of merit, but of grace. (a)

(a) Luke 17:10.

Q. 64.

But does not this doctrine make men careless and profane?

A.

By no means: for it is impossible that those, who are implanted into Christ by a true faith, should not bring forth fruits of thankfulness. (a)

(a) Matt.7:18; John 15:5.

OF THE SACRAMENTS

25. Lord's Day

Q. 65.

Since then we are made partakers of Christ and all his benefits by faith only, whence does this faith proceed?

A.

From the Holy Ghost, (a)

who works faith in our hearts by the preaching of the gospel, and confirms it by the use of the sacraments. (b)

(a) Eph.2:8,9; Eph.6:23; John 3:5; Philip.1:29. (b) Matt.28:19,20; 1 Pet.1:22,23.

Q. 66.

What are the sacraments?

A.

The sacraments are holy visible signs and seals, appointed of God for this end, that by the use thereof, he may the more fully declare and seal to us the promise of the gospel, viz., that he grants us freely the remission of sin, and life eternal, for the sake of that one sacrifice of Christ, accomplished on the cross. (a)

(a) Gen.17:11; Rom.4:11; Deut.30:6; Lev.6:25; Heb.9:7-9,24; Ezek.20:12; Isa.6:6,7; Isa.54:9.

Q. 67.

Are both word and sacraments, then, ordained and appointed for this end, that they may direct our faith to the sacrifice of Jesus Christ on the cross, as the only ground of our salvation? (a)

A.

Yes, indeed: for the Holy Ghost teaches us in the gospel, and assures us by the sacraments, that the whole of our salvation depends upon that one sacrifice of Christ which he offered for us on the cross.

(a) Rom.6:3; Gal.3:27.

Q. 68.

How many sacraments has Christ instituted in the new covenant, or testament?

A.

Two: namely, holy baptism, and the holy supper.

OF HOLY BAPTISM

26. Lord's Day

Q. 69.

How art thou admonished and assured by holy baptism, that the one sacrifice of Christ upon the cross is of real advantage to thee?

A.

Thus: That Christ appointed this external washing with water, (a)

adding thereto this promise, (b)

that I am as certainly washed by his blood and Spirit from all the pollution of my soul, that is, from all my sins, (c)

as I am washed externally with water, by which the filthiness of the body is commonly washed away.

(a) Matt.28:19. (b) Matt.28:19; Acts 2:38; Matt.3:11; Mark 16:16; John 1:33; Rom.6:3,4. (c) 1 Pet.3:21; Mark 1:4; Luke 3:3

Q. 70.

What is it to be washed with the blood and Spirit of Christ?

A.

It is to receive of God the remission of sins, freely, for the sake of Christ's blood, which he shed for us by his sacrifice upon the cross; (a)

and also to be renewed by the Holy Ghost, and sanctified to be members of Christ, that so we may more and more die unto sin, and lead holy and unblamable lives. (b)

(a) Heb.12:24; 1 Pet.1:2; Rev.1:5; Rev.7:14; Zech.13:1; Ezek.36:25.

(b) John 1:33; John 3:5; 1 Cor.6:11; 1 Cor.12:13; Rom.6:4; Col.2:12.

Q. 71.

Where has Christ promised us, that he will as certainly wash us by his blood and Spirit, as we are washed with the water of baptism?

A.

In the institution of baptism, which is thus expressed: "Go ye, therefore, and teach all nations, baptizing them in the name of the Father, and of the Son, and of the Holy Ghost", Matt.28:19.

And "he that believeth, and is baptized, shall be saved; but he that believeth not, shall be damned.", Mark 16:16.

This promise is also repeated, where the scripture calls baptism "the washing of regenerations" and the washing away of sins. Tit.3:5,

Acts 22:16. (a)

(a) Tit.3:5; Acts 22:16.

27. Lord's Day

Q. 72.

Is then the external baptism with water the washing away of sin itself?

A.

Not at all: (a)

for the blood of Jesus Christ only, and the Holy Ghost cleanse us from all sin. (b)

(a) Matt.3:11; 1 Pet.3:21; Eph.5:26,27. (b) 1 John 1:7; 1 Cor.6:11.

Q. 73.

Why then does the Holy Ghost call baptism "the washing of regeneration," and "the washing away of sins"?

A.

God speaks thus not without great cause, to-wit, not only thereby to teach us, that as the filth of the body is purged away by water, so our sins are removed by the blood and Spirit of Jesus Christ; (a)

but especially that by this divine pledge and sign he may assure us, that we are spiritually cleansed from our sins as really, as we are externally washed with water. (b)

(a) Rev.1:5; Rev.7:14; 1 Cor.6:11. (b) Mark 16:16; Gal.3:27.

Q. 74.

Are infants also to be baptized?

A.

Yes:

for since they, as well as the adult, are included in the covenant and church of God; (a)

and since redemption from sin (b)

by the blood of Christ, and the Holy Ghost, the author of faith, is promised to them no less than to the adult; (c)

they must therefore by baptism, as a sign of the covenant, be also admitted into the christian church; and be distinguished from the children of unbelievers (d)

as was done in the old covenant or testament by circumcision, (e)

instead of which baptism is instituted (f)

in the new covenant.

(a) Gen.17:7. (b) Matt.19:14. (c) Luke 1:15; Ps.22:10; Isa.44:1-3; Acts 2:39. (d) Acts 10:47. (e) Gen.17:14. (f) Col.2:11-13.

OF THE HOLY SUPPER OF OUR LORD JESUS CHRIST

28 Lord's Day

Q. 75.

How art thou admonished and assured in the Lord's Supper, that thou art a partaker of that one sacrifice of Christ, accomplished on the cross, and of all his benefits?

A.

Thus: That Christ has commanded me and all believers, to eat of this broken bread, and to drink of this cup, in remembrance of him, adding these promises: (a)

first, that his body was offered and broken on the cross for me, and his blood shed for me, as certainly as I see with my eyes, the bread of the Lord broken for me, and the cup communicated to me; and further, that he feeds and nourishes my soul to everlasting life, with his crucified body and shed blood, as assuredly as I receive from the hands of the minister, and taste with my mouth the bread and cup of the Lord, as certain signs of the body and blood of Christ.

(a) Matt.26:26-28; Mark 14:22-24; Luke 22:19,20; 1 Cor.10:16,17; 1 Cor.11:23-25; 1 Cor.12:13.

Q. 76.

What is it then to eat the crucified body, and drink the shed blood of Christ?

A.

It is not only to embrace with believing heart all the sufferings and death of Christ and thereby to obtain the pardon of sin, and life eternal; (a)

but also, besides that, to become more and more united to his sacred body, (b)

by the Holy Ghost, who dwells both in Christ and in us; so that we, though Christ is in heaven (c)

and we on earth, are notwithstanding "flesh of his flesh and bone of his bone" (d)

and that we live, and are governed forever by one spirit, (e)

as members of the same body are by one soul.

(a) John 6:35,40,47-54. (b) John 6:55,56. (c) Col.3:1; Acts 3:21; 1 Cor.11:26. (d) Eph.3:16; Eph.5:29,30,32; 1 Cor.6:15,17,19; 1 John 3:24; 1 John 4:13; John 14:23. (e) John 6:56-58; John 15:1-6; Eph.4:15,16.

Q. 77.

Where has Christ promised that he will as certainly feed and nourish believers with his body and bleed, as they eat of this broken bread, and drink of this cup?

A.

In the institution of the supper, which is thus expressed: (a)

"The Lord Jesus, the same night in which he was betrayed, took bread, and when he had given thanks, he brake it, and: said: eat, this is my body, which is broken for you; this do in remembrance of me. After the same manner also he took the cup, when he had supped, saying: this cup is the new testament in my blood; this do ye, as often as ye drink it, in remembrance of me.

For, as often as ye eat this bread, and drink this cup, ye do show the Lord's death till he come." 1 Cor.11:23-26.

This promise is repeated by the holy apostle Paul, where he says "The cup of blessing which we bless, is it not the communion of the blood of Christ? The bread which we break, is it not the communion of the body of Christ? For we being many are one bread, and one body: for we are all partakers of that one bread." 1 Cor.10:16,17.

(a) 1 Cor.11:23-25; Matt.26:26-28; Mark 14:22-24; Luke 22:19,20; 1 Cor.10:16,17.

29 Lord's Day

Q. 78.

Do then the bread and wine become the very body and blood of Christ?

A.

Not at all: (a)

but as the water in baptism is not changed into the blood of Christ, neither is the washing away of sin itself, being only the sign and confirmation thereof appointed of God; (b)

so the bread in the Lord's supper is not changed into the very body of Christ; (c)

though agreeably to the nature and properties of sacraments, (d)

it is called the body of Christ Jesus.

(a) Matt.26:29. (b) Eph.5:26; Tit.3:5. (c) Mark 14:24; 1 Cor.10:16,17,26-28. (d) Gen.17:10,11,14,19; Exod.12:11,13,27,43,48; Exod.13:9; 1 Pet.3:21; 1 Cor.10:1-4.

Q. 79.

Why then doth Christ call the bread "his body", and the cup "his blood", or "the new covenant in his blood"; and Paul the "communion of body and blood of Christ"?

A.

Christ speaks thus, not without great reason, namely, not only thereby to teach us, that as bread and wine support this temporal life, so his crucified body and shed blood are the true meat and drink, whereby our souls are fed to eternal life; (a)

but more especially by these visible signs and pledges to assure us, that we are as really partakers of his true body and blood by the operation of the Holy Ghost as we receive by the mouths of our bodies these holy signs in remembrance of him; (b)

and that all his sufferings and obedience are as certainly ours, as if we had in our own persons suffered and made satisfaction for our sins to God.

(a) John 6:51,55. (b) 1 Cor.10:16,17.

30. Lord's Day

Q. 80.

What difference is there between the Lord's supper and the popish mass?

A.

The Lord's supper testifies to us, that we have a full pardon of all sin by the only sacrifice of Jesus Christ, which he himself has once accomplished on the cross; (a)

and, that we by the Holy Ghost are ingrafted into Christ, (b)

who, according to his human nature is now not on earth, but in heaven, at the right hand of God his Father, (c)

and will there be worshipped by us. (d)

But the mass teaches, that the living and dead have not the pardon of sins through the sufferings of Christ, unless Christ is also daily offered for them by the priests; and further, that Christ is bodily under the form of bread and wine, and therefore is to be worshipped in them; so that the mass, at bottom, is nothing else than a denial of the one sacrifice and sufferings of Jesus Christ, and an accursed idolatry. (e)

(a) Heb.7:27; Heb.9:12,25-28; Heb.10:10,12-14; John 19:30; Matt.26:28; Luke 22:19,20. (b) 1 Cor.6:17; 1 Cor.10:16. (c) Heb.1:3; Heb.8:1,2; John 20:17. (d) Matt.6:20,21; John 4:21-24; Luke 24:52; Acts 7:55,56; Col.3:1; Philip.3:20,21; 1 Thess.1:10; Heb.9:6-10. (e) Heb.9:26; Heb.10:12,14,19-31.

Q. 81.

For whom is the Lord's supper instituted?

A.

For those who are truly sorrowful for their sins, and yet trust that these are forgiven them for the sake of Christ; and that their remaining infirmities are covered by his passion and death; and who also earnestly desire to have their faith more and more strengthened, and their lives more holy; but hypocrites, and such as turn not to God with sincere hearts, eat and drink judgment to themselves. (a)

(a) 1 Cor.10:19-22; 1 Cor.11:28,29.

Q. 82.

Are they also to be admitted to this supper, who, by confession and life, declare themselves unbelieving and ungodly?

A.

No; for by this, the covenant of God would be profaned, and his wrath kindled against the whole congregation; (a)

therefore it is the duty of the christian church, according to the appointment of Christ and his apostles, to exclude such persons, by the keys of the kingdom of heaven, till they show amendment of life.

(a) 1 Cor.11:20,34; Isa.1:11-15; Isa.66:3; Jer.7:21-23; Ps.50:16.

31. Lord's Day

Q. 83.

What are the keys of the kingdom of heaven?

A.

The preaching of the holy gospel, and christian discipline, or excommunication out of the christian church; by these two, the kingdom of heaven is opened to believers, and shut against unbelievers.

Q. 84.

How is the kingdom of heaven opened and shut by the preaching of the holy gospel?

A.

Thus: when according to the command of Christ, it is declared and publicly testified to all and every believer, that, whenever they receive the promise of the gospel by a true faith, all their sins are really forgiven them of God, for the sake of Christ's merits; and on the contrary, when it is declared and testified to all unbelievers, and such as do not sincerely repent, that they stand exposed to the wrath of God, and eternal condemnation, so long as they are unconverted: (a) according to which testimony of the gospel, God will judge them, both in this, and in the life to come.

(a) Matt.16:18,19; Matt.18:15-19; John 20:21-23.

Q. 85.

How is the kingdom of heaven shut and opened by christian discipline?

A.

Thus: when according to the command of Christ, those, who under the name of christians, maintain doctrines, or practices inconsistent therewith, and will not, after having been often brotherly admonished, renounce their errors and wicked course of life, are complained of to the church, or to those, who are thereunto appointed by the church; and if they despise their admonition, are by them forbidden the use of the sacraments; whereby they are excluded from the christian church, and by God himself from the kingdom of Christ; and when they promise and show real amendment, are again received as members of Christ and his church. (a)

(a) Matt.18:15-18; 1 Cor.5:2-5,11; 2 Thess.3:14,15; 2 Cor.2:6-8.

32. Lord's Day

Q. 86.

Since then we are delivered from our misery, merely of grace, through Christ, without any merit of ours, why must we still do good works?

A.

Because Christ, having redeemed and delivered us by his blood, also renews us by his Holy Spirit, after his own image; that so we may testify, by the whole of our conduct, our gratitude to God for his blessings, (a)

and that he may be praised by us; (b)

also, that every one may be assured in himself of his faith, (c)

by the fruits thereof; and that, by our godly conversation others may be gained to Christ. (d)

(a) Rom.6:13; Rom.12:1,2; 1 Pet.2:5,9,10; 1 Cor.6:20. (b) Matt.5:16; 1 Pet.2:12; 1 Pet.1:6,7. (c) 2 Pet.1:10; Matt.7:17; Gal.5:6,22,23. (d) 1 Pet.3:1,2; Rom.14:19.

Q. 87.

Cannot they then be saved, who, continuing in their wicked and ungrateful lives, are not converted to God?

A.

By no means; for the holy scripture declares that no unchaste person, idolater, adulterer, thief, covetous man, drunkard, slanderer, robber, or any such like, shall inherit the kingdom of God. (a)

(a) 1 Cor.6:9,10; Eph.5:5,6; 1 John 3:14.

33. Lord's Day

Q. 88.

Of how many parts does the true conversion of man consist?

A.

Of two parts; of the mortification of the old, and the quickening of the new man. (a)

(a) Rom.6:1,4-6; Eph.4:22-24; Col.3:5-10; 1 Cor.5:7; 2 Cor.7:10.

Q. 89.

What is the mortification of the old man?

A.

It is a sincere sorrow of heart, that we have provoked God by our sins; and more and more to hate and flee from them. (a)

(a) Rom.8:13; Joel 2:13; Hos.6:1.

Q. 90.

What is the quickening of the new man?

A.

It is a sincere joy of heart in God, through Christ, (a)

and with love and delight to live according to the will of God in all good works. (b)

(a) Rom.5:1; Rom.14:17; Isa.57:15. (b) Rom.6:10,11; Gal.2:20.

Q. 91.

But what are good works?

A.

Only those which proceed from a true faith, (a)

are performed according to the law of God, (b)

and to his glory; (c)

and not such as are founded on our imaginations, or the institutions of men. (d)

(a) Rom.14:23. (b) Lev.18:4; 1 Sam.15:22; Eph.2:10. (c) 1 Cor.10:31.

(d) Deut.12:32; Ezek.20:18,19; Isa.29:13; Matt.15:7-9.

34. Lord's Day

Q. 92.

What is the law of God?

A.

God spake all these words, Exodus 20:1-17 and Denteronomy 5:6-21, saying: I am the LORD thy God, which have brought thee out of the land of Egypt, out of the house of bondage.

1st commandment:

Thou shalt have no other gods before me.

2nd commandment:

Thou shalt not make unto thee any graven image, or any likeness of any thing that is in heaven above, or that is in the earth beneath, or that is in the water under the earth. Thou shalt not bow down thyself to them, nor serve them; for I the LORD thy God am a jealous God, visiting the iniquity of the fathers upon the children unto the third and fourth generation of them that hate me, and shewing mercy unto thousands of them that love me, and keep my commandments.

3rd commandment:

Thou shalt not take the name of the LORD thy God in vain; for the LORD will not hold him guiltless that taketh his name in vain.

4th commandment:

Remember the sabbath day, to keep it holy. Six days shalt thou labour, and do all thy work; but the seventh day is the sabbath of the LORD thy God: in it thou shalt not do any work, thou, nor thy son, nor thy daughter, thy manservant, nor thy maidservant, nor thy cattle, nor thy stranger that is within thy gates. For in six days the LORD made heaven and earth, the sea, and all that in them is, and rested the seventh day: wherefore the LORD blessed the sabbath day, and hallowed it.

5th commandment:

Honour thy father and thy mother: that thy days may be long upon the land which the LORD thy God giveth thee.

6th commandment:

Thou shalt not kill.

7th commandment:

Thou shalt not commit adultery.

8th commandment:

Thou shalt not steal.

9th commandment:

Thou shalt not bear false witness against thy neighbour.

10th commandment:

Thou shalt not covet thy neighbour's house, thou shalt not covet thy neighbour's wife, nor his manservant, nor his maidservant, nor his ox, nor his ass, nor any thing that is thy neighbour's.

Q. 93.

How are these commandments divided?

A.

Into two tables; (a)

the first of which teaches us how we must behave towards God; the second, what duties we owe to our neighbour. (b)

(a) Exod.34:28; Deut.4:13; Deut.10:3,4. (b) Matt.22:37-40.

Q. 94.

What does God enjoin in the first commandment?

A.

That I, as sincerely as I desire the salvation of my own soul, avoid and flee from all idolatry, (a)

sorcery, soothsaying, superstition, (b)

invocation of saints, or any other creatures; (c)

and learn rightly to know the only true God; (d)

trust in him alone, (e)

with humility (f)

and patience submit to him; (g)

expect all good things from him only; (h)

love, (i)
fear, (j)
and glorify him with my whole heart; (k)
so that I renounce and forsake all creatures, rather than commit even the least thing contrary to his will. (l)
(a) 1 John 5:21; 1 Cor.6:9,10; 1 Cor.10:7,14. (b) Lev.19:31; Deut.18:9-12. (c) Matt.4:10; Rev.19:10; Rev.22:8,9. (d) John 17:3. (e) Jer.17:5,7. (f) 1 Pet.5:5,6. (g) Heb.10:36; Col.1:11; Rom.5:3,4; 1 Cor.10:10; Philip.2:14. (h) Ps.104:27-30; Isa.45:7; James 1:17. (i) Deut.6:5; Matt.22:37. (j) Deut.6:2; Ps.111:10; Prov.1:7; Prov.9:10; Matt.10:28. (k) Matt.4:10; Deut.10:20,21. (l) Matt.5:29,30; Matt.10:37; Acts 5:29.

Q. 95.
What is idolatry?
A.
Idolatry is, instead of, or besides that one true God, who has manifested himself in his word, to contrive, or have any other object, in which men place their trust. (a)
(a) Eph.5:5; 1 Chron.16:26; Philip.3:19; Gal.4:8; Eph.2:12; 1 John 2:23; 2 John 1:9; John 5:23.

35. Lord's Day

Q. 96.
What does God require in the second commandment?
A.
That we in no wise represent God by images, (a)
nor worship him in any other way than he has commanded in his word. (b)
(a) Deut.4:15-19; Isa.40:18-25; Rom.1:23,24; Acts 17:29. (b) 1 Sam.15:23; Deut.12:30-32; Matt.15:9.

Q. 97.
Are images then not at all to be made?
A.
God neither can, nor may be represented by any means: (a)
but as to creatures; though they may be represented, yet God forbids to make, or have any resemblance of them, either in order to worship them or to serve God by them. (b)
(a) Isa.40:25. (b) Exod.23:24,25; Exod.34:13,14,17; Num.33:52; Deut.7:5; Deut.12:3; Deut.16:21; 2 Kin.18:3,4.

Q. 98.

But may not images be tolerated in the churches, as books to the laity?

A.

No: for we must not pretend to be wiser than God, who will have his people taught, not by dumb images, (a)

but by the lively preaching of his word. (b)

(a) Jer.10:8; Hab.2:18,19. (b) Rom.10:14,15,17; 2 Pet.1:19; 2 Tim.3:16,17.

36. Lord's Day

Q. 99.

What is required in the third commandment?

A.

That we, not only by cursing (a)

or perjury, (b)

but also by rash swearing, (c)

must not profane or abuse the name of God; nor by silence or connivance be partakers of these horrible sins in others; (d)

and, briefly, that we use the holy name of God no otherwise than with fear and reverence; (e)

so that he may be rightly confessed (f)

and worshipped by us, (g)

and be glorified in all our words and works. (h)

(a) Lev.24:11-16. (b) Lev.19:12. (c) Matt.5:37; James 5:12. (d) Lev.5:1; Prov.29:24. (e) Jer.4:2; Isa.45:23. (f) Rom.10:9,10; Matt.10:32. (g) Ps.50:15; 1 Tim.2:8. (h) Rom.2:24; 1 Tim.6:1; Col.3:16,17.

Q. 100.

Is then the profaning of God's name, by swearing and cursing, so heinous a sin, that his wrath is kindled against those who do not endeavour, as much as in them lies, to prevent and forbid such cursing and swearing?

A.

It undoubtedly is, (a)

for there is no sin greater or more provoking to God, than the profaning of his name; and therefore he has commanded this sin to be punished with death. (b)

(a) Prov.29:24; Lev.5:1. (b) Lev.24:15,16.

37. Lord's Day

Q. 101.

May we then swear religiously by the name of God?

A.

Yes: either when the magistrates demand it of the subjects; or when necessity requires us thereby to confirm a fidelity and truth to the glory of God, and the safety of our neighbour: for such an oath is founded on God's word, (a)

and therefore was justly used by the saints, both in the Old and New Testament. (b)

(a) Deut.6:13; Deut.10:20; Isa.48:1; Heb.6:16. (b) Gen.21:24; Gen.31:53,54; Jos.9:15,19; 1 Sam.24:22; 2 Sam.3:35; 1 Kin.1:28-30; Rom.1:9; 2 Cor.1:23.

Q. 102.

May we also swear by saints or any other creatures?

A.

No; for a lawful oath is calling upon God, as the only one who knows the heart, that he will bear witness to the truth, and punish me if I swear falsely; (a)

which honour is due to no creature. (b)

(a) 2 Cor.1:23; Rom.9:1. (b) Matt.5:34-36; James 5:12.

38. Lord's Day

Q. 103.

What does God require in the fourth commandment?

A.

First, that the ministry of the gospel and the schools be maintained; (a)

and that I, especially on the sabbath, that is, on the day of rest, diligently frequent the church of God, (b)

to hear his word, (c)

to use the sacraments, (d)

publicly to call upon the Lord, (e)

and contribute to the relief of the poor. (f)

Secondly, that all the days of my life I cease from my evil works, and yield myself to the Lord, to work by his Holy Spirit in me: and thus begin in this life the eternal sabbath. (g)

(a) Tit.1:5; 2 Tim.3:14,15; 1 Tim.5:17; 1 Cor.9:11,13,14; 2 Tim.2:2. (b) Ps.40:10,11; Ps.68:27; Acts 2:42,46. (c) 1 Tim.4:13,19; 1 Cor.14:29,31. (d) 1 Cor.11:33. (e) 1 Tim.2:1-3,8-11; 1 Cor.14:16. (f) 1 Cor.16:2. (g) Isa.66:23.

39. Lord's Day

Q. 104.

What does God require in the fifth commandment?

A.

That I show all honour, love and fidelity, to my father and mother, and all in authority over me, and submit myself to their good instruction and correction, with due obedience; (a)

and also patiently bear with their weaknesses and infirmities, (b)

since it pleases God to govern us by their hand. (c)

(a) Eph.5:22; Eph.6:1-5; Col.3:18,20-24; Prov.1:8; Prov.4:1; Prov.15:20; Prov.20:20; Exod.21:17; Rom.13:1-7. (b) Prov.23:22; Gen.9:24,25; 1 Pet.2:18. (c) Eph.6:4,9; Col.3:19-21; Rom.13:2,3; Matt.22:21.

40. Lord's Day

Q. 105.

What does God require in the sixth commandment?

A.

That neither in thoughts, nor words, nor gestures, much less in deeds, I dishonour, hate, wound, or kill my neighbour, by myself or by another: (a)

but that I lay aside all desire of revenge: (b)

also, that I hurt not myself, nor wilfully expose myself to any danger. (c)

Wherefore also the magistrate is armed with the sword, to prevent murder. (d)

(a) Matt.5:21,22; Matt.26:52; Gen.9:6. (b) Eph.4:26; Rom.12:19; Matt.5:25; Matt.18:35. (c) Rom.13:14; Col.2:23; Matt.4:7. (d) Gen.9:6; Exod.21:14; Matt.26:52; Rom.13:4.

Q. 106.

But this commandment seems only to speak of murder?

A.

In forbidding murder, God teaches us, that he abhors the causes thereof, such as envy, (a)

hatred, (b)

anger, (c)

and desire of revenge; and that he accounts all these as murder. (d)

(a) Prov.14:30; Rom.1:29. (b) 1 John 2:9,11. (c) James 1:20; Gal.5:19,21. (d) 1 John 3:15.

Q. 107.

But is it enough that we do not kill any man in the manner mentioned above?

A.

No: for when God forbids envy, hatred, and anger, he commands us to love our neighbour as ourselves; (a)

to show patience, peace, meekness, mercy, and all kindness, towards him, (b)

and prevent his hurt as much as in us lies; (c)

and that we do good, even to our enemies. (d)

(a) Matt.7:12; Matt.22:39; Rom.12:10. (b) Eph.4:2; Gal.6:1,2; Matt.5:5,7,9; Rom.12:18; Luke 6:36; 1 Pet.3:8; Col.3:12; Rom.12:10,15. (c) Exod.23:5. (d) Matt.5:44,45; Rom.12:20,21.

41. Lord's Day

Q. 108.

What does the seventh commandment teach us?

A.

That all uncleanness is accursed of God: (a)

and that therefore we must with all our hearts detest the same, (b)

and live chastely and temperately, (c)

whether in holy wedlock, or in single life. (d)

(a) Lev.18:27,28. (b) Jude 1:23. (c) 1 Thess.4:3-5. (d) Heb.13:4; 1 Cor.7:7-9,27.

Q. 109.

Does God forbid in this commandment, only adultery, and such like gross sins?

A.

Since both our body and soul are temples of the holy Ghost, he commands us to preserve them pure and holy: therefore he forbids all unchaste actions, gestures, words, (a)

thoughts, desires, (b)

and whatever can entice men thereto. (c)

(a) Eph.5:3,4; 1 Cor.6:18-20. (b) Matt.5:27,28. (c) Eph.5:18; 1 Cor.15:33.

42. Lord's Day

Q. 110.

What does God forbid in the eighth commandment?

A.

God forbids not only those thefts, (a)

and robberies, (b)

which are punishable by the magistrate; but he comprehends under the name of theft all wicked tricks and devices, whereby we design to appropriate to ourselves the goods which belong to our neighbour: (c)

whether it be by force, or under the appearance of right, as by unjust weights, ells, measures, fraudulent merchandise, (d)

false coins, usury, (e)

or by any other way forbidden by God; as also all covetousness, (f)

all abuse and waste of his gifts. (g)

(a) 1 Cor.6:10. (b) 1 Cor.5:10; Isa.33:1. (c) Luke 3:14; 1 Thess.4:6. (d) Prov.11:1; Prov.16:11; Ezek.45:9-12; Deut.25:13-16. (e) Ps.15:5; Luke 6:35. (f) 1 Cor.6:10. (g) Prov.23:20,21; Prov.21:20.

Q. 111.

But what does God require in this commandment?

A.

That I promote the advantage of my neighbour in every instance I can or may; and deal with him as I desire to be dealt with by others: (a)

further also that I faithfully labour, so that I may be able to relieve the needy. (b)

(a) Matt.7:12. (b) Eph.4:28.

43. Lord's Day

Q. 112.

What is required in the ninth commandment?

A.

That I bear false witness against no man, (a)

nor falsify any man's words; (b)

that I be no backbiter, nor slanderer; (c)

that I do not judge, nor join in condemning any man rashly, or unheard; (d)

but that I avoid all sorts of lies and deceit, as the proper works of the devil, (e)

unless I would bring down upon me the heavy wrath of God; (f)

likewise, that in judgment and all other dealings I love the truth, speak it uprightly and confess it; (g)

also that I defend and promote, as much as I am able, the horror and good character of my neighbour. (h)

(a) Prov.19:5,9; Prov.21:28. (b) Ps.15:3; Ps.50:19,20. (c) Rom.1:29,30. (d) Matt.7:1,2; Luke 6:37. (e) John 8:44. (f) Prov.12:22; Prov.13:5. (g) 1 Cor.13:6; Eph.4:25. (h) 1 Pet.4:8.

44. Lord's Day

Q. 113.

What does the tenth commandment require of us?

A.

That even the smallest inclination or thought, contrary to any of God's commandments, never rise in our hearts; but that at all times we hate all sin with our whole heart, and delight in all righteousness. (a)

(a) Rom.7:7.

Q. 114.

But can those who are converted to God perfectly keep these commandments?

A.

No: but even the holiest men, while in this life, have only a small beginning of this obedience; (a)

yet so, that with a sincere resolution they begin to live, not only according to some, but all the commandments of God. (b)

(a) 1 John 1:8-10; Rom.7:14,15; Eccl.7:20; 1 Cor.13:9. (b) Rom.7:22; Ps.1:2; James 2:10.

Q. 115.

Why will God then have the ten commandments so strictly preached, since no man in this life can keep them?

A.

First, that all our lifetime we may learn more and more to know (a)

our sinful nature, and thus become the more earnest in seeking the remission of sin, and righteousness in Christ; (b)

likewise, that we constantly endeavour and pray to God for the grace of the Holy Spirit, that we may become more and more conformable to the image of God, till we arrive at the perfection proposed to us, in a life to come. (c)

(a) Rom.3:20; 1 John 1:9; Ps.32:5. (b) Matt.5:6; Rom.7:24,25. (c) 1 Cor.9:24; Philip.3:11-14.

45. Lord's Day

Q. 116.

Why is prayer necessary for christians?

A.

Because it is the chief part of thankfulness which God requires of us: (a) and also, because God will give his grace and Holy Spirit to those only, who with sincere desires continually ask them of him, and are thankful for them. (b)

(a) Ps.50:14,15. (b) Matt.7:7,8; Luke 11:9,10,13; 1 Thess.5:17.

Q. 117.

What are the requisites of that prayer, which is acceptable to God, and which he will hear?

A.

First, that we from the heart pray (a)

to the one true God only, who has manifested himself in his word, (b)

for all things, he has commanded us to ask of him; (c)

secondly, that we rightly and thoroughly know our need and misery, (d)

that so we may deeply humble ourselves in the presence of his divine majesty; (e)

thirdly, that we be fully persuaded that he, notwithstanding that we are unworthy of it, will, for the sake of Christ our Lord, certainly hear our prayer, (f)

as he has promised us in his word. (g)

(a) John 4:24; Ps.145:18. (b) Rev.19:10; John 4:22-24. (c) Rom.8:26; 1 John 5:14; James 1:5. (d) 2 Chron.20:12. (e) Ps.2:11; Ps.34:19; Isa.66:2. (f) Rom.10:14; James 1:6. (g) John 14:13,14; John 16:23; Dan.9:17,18. (h) Matt.7:8; Ps.27:8.

Q. 118.

What has God commanded us to ask of him?

A.

All things necessary for soul and body; (a)

which Christ our Lord has comprised in that prayer he himself has taught us.

(a) James 1:17; Matt.6:33.

Q. 119.

What are the words of that prayer? (a)

A.

Our Father which art in heaven,
1 Hallowed be thy name.
2 Thy kingdom come.
3 Thy will be done on earth, as it is in heaven.
4 Give us this day our daily bread.
5 And forgive us our debts, as we forgive our debtors.
6 And lead us not into temptation, but deliver us from evil.
For thine is the kingdom, and the power, and the glory, for ever.
Amen.

(a) Matt.6:9-13; Luke 11:2-4.

46. Lord's Day

Q. 120.

Why has Christ commanded us to address God thus: "Our Father"?

A.

That immediately, in the very beginning of our prayer, he might excite in us a childlike reverence for, and confidence in God, which are the foundation of our prayer: namely, that God is become our Father in Christ, and will much less deny us what we ask of him in true faith, than our parents will refuse us earthly things. (a)

(a) Matt.7:9-11; Luke 11:11-13.

Q. 121.

Why is it here added, "Which art in heaven"?

A.

Lest we should form any earthly conceptions of God's heavenly majesty, (a)

and that we may expect from his almighty power all things necessary for soul and body. (b)

(a) Jer.23:23,24; Acts 17:24,25,27. (b) Rom.10:12.

47. Lord's Day

Q. 122.

Which is the first petition?

A.

"Hallowed be thy name"; that is, grant us, first, rightly to know thee, (a)

and to sanctify, glorify and praise thee, (b)

in all thy works, in which thy power, wisdom, goodness, justice, mercy and truth, are clearly displayed; and further also, that we may so order and direct our whole lives, our thoughts, words and actions, that thy name may never be blasphemed, but rather honoured and praised on our account. (c)

(a) John 17:3; Jer.9:24; Jer.31:33,34; Matt.16:17; James 1:5; Ps.119:105. (b) Ps.119:137; Luke 1:46,47,68,69; Rom.11:33-36. (c) Ps.71:8; Ps.115:1.

48. Lord's Day

Q. 123.

Which is the second petition?

A.

"Thy kingdom come"; that is, rule us so by thy word and Spirit, that we may submit ourselves more and more to thee; (a)

preserve and increase thy church; (b)

destroy the works of the devil, and all violence which would exalt itself against thee; and also all wicked counsels devised against thy holy word; (c)

till the full perfection of thy kingdom take place, (d)

wherein thou shalt be all in all. (e)

(a) Matt.6:33; Ps.119:5; Ps.143:10. (b) Ps.51:18; Ps.122:6-9. (c) 1 John 3:8; Rom.16:20. (d) Rev.22:17,20; Rom.8:22,23. (e) 1 Cor.15:28.

49. Lord's Day

Q. 124.

Which is the third petition?

A.

"Thy will be done on earth as it is in heaven"; that is, grant that we and all men may renounce our own will, (a)

and without murmuring obey thy will, which is only good; (b)

that every one may attend to, and perform the duties of his station and calling, (c)

as willingly and faithfully as the angels do in heaven. (d)

(a) Matt.16:24; Tit.2:11,12. (b) Luke 22:42; Eph.5:10; Rom.12:2. (c) 1 Cor.7:24. (d) Ps.103:20,21.

50. Lord's Day

Q. 125.

Which is the fourth petition?

A.

"Give us this day our daily bread"; that is, be pleased to provide us with all things necessary for the body, (a) that we may thereby acknowledge thee to be the only fountain of all good, (b)

and that neither our care nor industry, nor even thy gifts, can profit us without thy blessing; (c)

and therefore that we may withdraw our trust from all creatures, and place it alone in thee. (d)

(a) Ps.104:27,28; Ps.145:15,16; Matt.6:25,26. (b) James 1:17; Acts 14:17; Acts 17:27,28. (c) 1 Cor.15:58; Deut.8:3; Ps.37:3-5,16; Ps.127:1,2. (d) Ps.55:23; Ps.62:11; Ps.146:3; Jer.17:5,7.

51. Lord's Day

Q. 126.

Which is the fifth petition?

A.

"And forgive us our debts as we forgive our debtors"; that is, be pleased for the sake of Christ's blood, not to impute to us poor sinners, our transgressions, nor that depravity, which always cleaves to us; (a)

even as we feel this evidence of thy grace in us, that it is our firm resolution from the heart to forgive our neighbour. (b)

(a) Ps.51:1-7; Ps.143:2; 1 John 2:1,2; Rom.8:1. (b) Matt.6:14,15.

52. Lord's Day

Q. 127.

Which is the sixth petition?

A.

"And lead us not into temptation, but deliver us from evil"; that is, since we are so weak in ourselves, that we cannot stand a moment; (a)

and besides this, since our mortal enemies, the devil, (b)

the world, (c)

and our own flesh, (d)

cease not to assault us,

do thou therefore preserve and strengthen us by the power of thy Holy Spirit, that we may not be overcome in this spiritual warfare, (e)

but constantly and strenuously may resist our foes, till at last we obtain a complete victory. (f)

(a) John 15:5; Ps.103:14. (b) 1 Pet.5:8; Eph.6:12. (c) John 15:19. (d) Rom.7:23; Gal.5:17. (e) Matt.26:41; Mark 13:33. (f) 1 Thess.3:13; 1 Thess.5:23.

Q. 128.

How dost thou conclude thy prayer?

A.

"For thine is the kingdom, and the power, and the glory, forever"; that is, all these we ask of thee, because thou, being our King and almighty, art willing and able to give us all good; (a)

and all this we pray for, that thereby not we, but thy holy name, may be glorified for ever. (b)

(a) Rom.10:11,12; 2 Pet.2:9. (b) John 14:13; Jer.33:8,9; Ps.115:1.

Q. 129.

What does the word "Amen" signify?

A.

"Amen" signifies, it shall truly and certainly be: for my prayer is more assuredly heard of God, than I feel in my heart that I desire these things of him. (a)

(a) 2 Cor.1:20; 2 Tim.2:13.

Made in the USA
Middletown, DE
12 August 2020